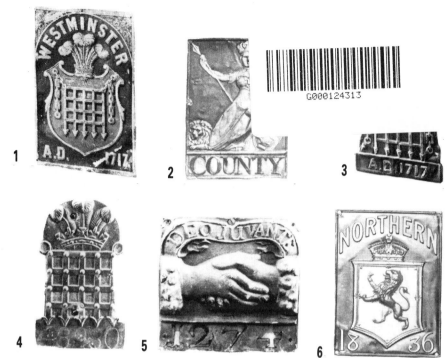

1, 3: *Plates of the Westminster Fire Office, which used the Black Prince's feathers and the portcullis favoured by Henry VII.* **4:** *Mark of the Westminster showing policy number at the base.* **2:** *County Fire Office (1807-1906). The early plates show Britannia holding a Hanoverian shield. This later became the Royal Arms of Victoria and then the Union flag.* **5:** *Mark of the Friendly Insurance Society of Edinburgh (1720). The motto above the clasped hands means 'with God's help'.* **6:** *Plate of the Northern showing the lion rampant of the Scottish royal arms.*

COVER: *A plate of the County Fire Office, established in 1807, from the building of the Bucks and Oxon Union Bank, Market Square, Aylesbury, and now in the Buckinghamshire County Museum, Aylesbury.*

FIRE-MARKS

John Vince

Shire Publications Ltd

CONTENTS

Set in 9 on 9 point Times and printed in Great Britain by C. I. Thomas & Sons (Haverfordwest) Ltd, Press Buildings, Merlins Bridge, Haverfordwest.

Details of the fire-hook at Ivinghoe, Buckinghamshire.

ABOVE: *A manual engine of the Royal Company made by the famous firm of Shand Mason. Note the helmets and buckets in the showcase. (Chartered Insurance Institute.)*

BEGINNINGS

Fire has always been a hazard to the householder. In the days when most English dwellings had roofs of thatch, fires were catastrophic and spread quickly from rooftop to rooftop. Large areas of a town or village could be reduced to ashes very quickly. Before the days of the local fire brigade each parish had to fend for itself, and in the seventeenth century most had little more than a few fire buckets and a fire-hook by way of protection. These were kept in a prominent place such as the church or town hall.

The invention of an 'engine' to fight fires marked an important stage in man's continuing battle against the flames. An appliance built by Hautch at Nurnberg in 1657 seems to have been the first mechanical device. In 1672 a flexible hose was invented by Jan Vanderheide. Newsham patented an engine in 1700 and his design seems to have influenced engine makers for over a century. The introduction of steam engines provided firemen with more power than they had ever been able to generate with the old Newsham-type hand pumps.

England's most famous fire, the Great Fire of London, started on 2nd September 1666 and raged for three days and nights. Its course was finally stopped when houses were blown up to prevent

ABOVE: *Part of the frieze showing the Great Fire of London (1666), painted by C. Walter Hodges in the Chartered Insurance Institute's museum.*

the flames from jumping across the narrow city streets. Over thirteen thousand houses in some four hundred streets were laid waste. Among the public buildings destroyed were the Guildhall, the Royal Exchange, the Custom House, eighty-nine churches and St Paul's Cathedral. The extent of the human suffering could scarcely be calculated but one effect of this disaster was to hasten the development of the concept of insurance.

One of the earliest methods of sharing the risk of loss of property was to form a group of people into a contributorship. Each member carried a fixed portion of the total risk. A group of ten could contract to bear a risk of £10 each; and if any member suffered a loss of up to £100 he could collect the portion due to him from each individual. The method was cumbersome and was probably subject to delay at a time when the unfortunate

member desired a speedy settlement. From these primitive arrangements evolved the method by which an insurer paid a premium related to the value of his goods or property.

The early societies formed for the protection of their members often incorporated the words 'mutual' or 'friendly' into their titles. In 1683 William Hale of Kings Walden, Hertfordshire, was a co-founder of the office with the oldest known mark, the Friendly Society of London. The Hand-in-Hand office was established in 1696 and was also known as the Amicable Contributionship. During the eighteenth and nineteenth centuries there was a great expansion in the number of companies offering fire insurance and the signs they devised are considered below. The smaller companies were frequently taken over by larger ones even in the nineteenth century.

4

LEFT: *A panel at the base of Wren's Monument to the Great Fire of London.*

BELOW LEFT: *A sundial erected on a house in Stony Stratford, Buckinghamshire, to commemorate a fire that destroyed much of the town.*

BELOW RIGHT: *The monument at Blandford Forum, Dorset, commemorating the rebuilding of the town after a disastrous fire in 1760.*

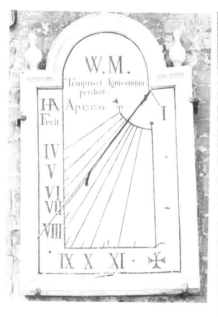

7, 8: *Plates of the Patriotic Assurance Company of Ireland (Dublin, 1824).* 9: *The allegorical figure of patriotism appears on this variant, comforting a woman and child.*

THE FIRST FIRE-MARKS

One of the problems facing an insurance company in the old days was the accurate identification of insured property. Precise addresses are relatively modern. Until the postal service began to expand in the 1840s there was little need for houses to be numbered. When an address was only a vague form of identification the insurance companies had to guard against fraud. Care had to be taken to identify protected properties and the adoption of company fire-marks by the early fire offices helped to distinguish the premises they insured. These early marks usually bear a number below the company's device, indicating the policy relating to the building. In larger towns a fire-mark also helped members of the company's fire brigade to identify their responsibilities. Fire-marks also served to advertise a

10: *A damaged plate of the Aegus Fire and Life Company (1825). The Gorgon's head was borrowed from the shield of the Greek god Zeus.* 11, 12: *Variants of the Protector Company (1825) showing a fireman with old Westminster Bridge in the background.*

13: *Plate of the Royal Irish Company (Dublin, 1823-7). The lion and the unicorn support the Hanoverian royal arms.* **14:** *Plate of the Shamrock Company (Dublin, 1823-5).* **15:** *Plate of the Alliance (1824) showing a castle as a symbol of strength.*

company's services and they represent some of the earliest examples of the advertiser's art. The bright colours were used to attract the eyes of passers-by as well as the company's firemen.

Tales of firemen arriving to find a blazing building bearing the mark of another 'office' and sitting down to watch it reduced to ashes are entirely apocryphal. There is considerable evidence to show that the different brigades rendered assistance to each other. The co-operation of the principal private brigades led to the formation of the London Fire Engine Establishment in 1833. This establishment became a public concern in 1866 when it was taken over by the Metropolitan Board of Works. The splendid traditions of our modern fire service are derived from the loyal and trusted servants employed by the private companies in Georgian and Victorian England. The first London firemen were mostly watermen. There was good cause to have firemen at hand along the water-front where valuable merchandise was at

16: *North British and Mercantile plate which impales the civic arms of Edinburgh and London.* **17:** *Another variant of the North British, which portrays St George and the dragon.* **18:** *A Bristol Union (1818) plate with the company's emblem, a bundle of faggots.*

19: *Mark number 253 of the Newcastle upon Tyne Fire Office (1783). The three castles are derived from the city arms.* 20: *A plate from the same company which bears its name instead of a policy number.* 21: *Mark 16 of the Worcester Fire Office (1790) with the city arms. On the scroll at the base appears the motto: Civitas in Bello in Pace Fidelis. See also 77.*

risk. Firemen were held in such high regard that they enjoyed immunity from the powers of the dreaded press gangs which until 1853 provided so many reluctant mariners for the Royal Navy.

The first insurers were men of property. With the passage of time insurance cover crept down the social scale and even those with modest possessions began to take an interest in its advantages. Some companies issued special marks to show that goods were insured as well as property. Once the idea of insurance had been established in London, companies began to extend their business to other places. Certain towns were favoured with a company fire brigade; but a large volume of business was transacted in towns and villages where insurers simply enjoyed a financial protection. Old county directories show just how well fire offices advertised and how many agents existed, even in the most remote corners of the land.

22-24: *Three Norwich Union (1797) plates with subtle variations. This company issued twenty-one variants.*

25   **26**   **27**

25: *Very little is known about the Fife Company. The laurel leaves are derived from the civic arms of Cupar, the county town.* **26:** *Plate of the Essex and Suffolk Equitable Insurance Society (Colchester, 1802). The shield displays the county arms of Essex.* **27:** *Mark 138, issued 1st March 1803, of the Kent Fire Insurance Company. The horse salient comes from the Saxon white horse emblem that appears in the county arms. See also 34, 35, 36.*

FIRE-MARKS AND PLATES

Ever since men began to build houses they have favoured amulets of one kind or another in an effort to keep trouble from the door: animal bones built into the walls; sun-snake symbols carved in the granite lintels of Dartmoor doorways; 'hag stones' suspended inside the byre door; rowan trees planted in so many country gardens. Whoever had the idea of providing a visible symbol to add comfort to the insurer's abstract 'cover' certainly knew something of psychology and probably about folklore. Can it really be a coincidence that William Hale should have chosen a serpent (a sun-snake) as part of the device used by the

28: *Plate of the Leeds and Yorkshire Company (1824). The fleece is derived from the Leeds city arms.* **29, 30:** *Two plates of the Manchester Fire Insurance Company. The civic shield of Manchester provides the device.*

28   **29**   **30**

31: *The St Patrick Insurance Company (Dublin, 1824-9).* 32, 33: *Plates of the Yorkshire Insurance Company (1824) which show different views of York Minster's west end.*

Friendly Society of London? The choice of the sun emblem by the Sun Fire Office may not simply be an allusion to the element fire. The sun-disc was a device of extreme antiquity and its use was commonplace as a horse ornament two centuries ago. Few emblems were thought to possess as much power to reflect the 'evil eye'. The apparent success of the Sun Fire Office in the countryside may in part be attributed to the support it derived from folklore.

At first sight fire-marks present a confusing array of designs. Those with a sense of history will want to start with the oldest and progress to the latest.

Various materials were used but the oldest, and numbered, marks were usually made of lead. In the early 1800s copper was favoured. Iron and tin came into use

34-36: *Three more variants of the Kent Insurance Company See also 27.*

37, 38: *Two variants of the Norwich Union showing the seated figure of Justice. Note the difference in their respective sizes. Plates of this shape are often called 'keyholes'.* **39:** *Another variant with Justice standing. See also 22, 23, 24.*

about 1820-5.

The first fire office was established in 1680 by Dr Nicholas Barbon. In 1705 it adopted the name Phenix Office but it did not endure and seems to have ceased business before the 1720s. Many *Phoenix* marks and plates may still be seen. They belong, however, to a new company which was founded in London in 1782.

Collectors of fire-marks distinguish between 'marks' bearing a policy number and those which simply show a company's emblem. The latter are known to the purist as 'plates'. Some companies issued marks or plates for almost two hundred years. Designs varied in detail over the years and the collector uses the term 'variant' to distinguish them. The Sun Fire Office (established in 1710) has twenty-six variants.

40-42: *Plates of the British Fire Office (1799) show the lion in different attitudes.*

40   **41**   **42**

43, 44: *Plates of the Lancashire Insurance Company (1852) which make use of the heraldic lions borne by John of Gaunt, Duke of Lancaster.* **46-48:** *The London and Lancashire Insurance Company (1862) should not be confused with the Lancashire. Note the use of borrowed heraldic arms once again.* **45:** *The Queen Insurance Company was established in Liverpool in 1857. Two more of its five variants are shown below (91, 93).*

Keyhole marks and plates: **49-52, 56:** *The plates of the Phoenix Assurance Company (1782) can be found in many parts of Britain. There are fifteen variants. On the earlier marks the motto 'Protection' often appears at the base of the oval. The plates display interesting variations in the lettering used — 52 is particu-*

larly good — and some omit the spear behind the oval. **53:** *The plate derived from the marks 123 and 124.* **54:** *A variation on 15 above.* **55, 58:** *Two of the five variants of the Hibernian Fire Insurance Company, the oldest Irish fire office, which was established in Dublin in 1771. These marks are very similar to some variants of the Royal Exchange: see also 177-9 and compare them with 188.* **57, 59:** *The Hope Fire and Life Assurance Company (1807) adopted the anchor as its emblem. This company should not be confused with the Anchor Fire Office (1808) or the Anchor Fire and Life Insurance Company (1849).* **60-61:** *Norwich Union (1797) plates. See also 105, 151.* **62:** *A Norwich General Assurance Office (1792) mark with distinctive emblems that should not be confused with 60 or 61.*

49

50

51

52

53

54

55

56

57

58

59

60

61

62

63

64

65

66

67

68

63: *An Equitable plate (1873) with a standing figure of Justice.* **64-65:** *The two variants of the National (1878).* **66:** *The name of the Palatine Insurance Company (Manchester, 1886-1900) takes us back to the Roman era. Roman emperors lived on the slopes of the Mons Palatinus. Thus the word 'palace' has become attached to all royal households. The counties palatine of Chester, Durham and Lancaster derive their titles from the delegated regal authority, the 'jura regalia', once exercised by the Earls of Chester, the Bishops of Durham and the Dukes of Lancaster. Similar palatine rights were once possessed by Pembroke and Hexham. See also 115.* **67:** *A regal head to be compared with 45 and 91.* **68:** *Windmills were a special fire risk, as millstones could overheat if neglected and could easily start a fire. The National British and Irish Millers' Insurance Company (London, 1896-1918) provides two unusual and picturesque variants. See also 156.* **69, 71:** *On the plates of the Liverpool, London*

and Globe are the emblems collected by its amalgamations. The company was established as the Liverpool Fire Office in 1836. Ten years later it absorbed the London, Edinburgh and Dublin and changed its title to the Liverpool and London Fire and Life Insurance Company. When it took over the Globe (see 134-6) it added the last element to its name. **70:** *Northern Assurance Company. See also 6.* **72:** *See 15 and 54.* **73, 74:** *The two variants of an office established at Chelmsford in 1824.* **75, 84:** *Two variants of the Hertfordshire, Cambridgeshire and County Fire Office (1824-31).* **76:** *The only variant of the East Kent and Canterbury Economic Fire Assurance Association.* **77:** *Worcester Fire Office. See also 21.* **78:** *A Bristol mark. See 131.* **79, 80, 85:** *Plates of the District Office (1834-64).* **81:** *See 7.* **82:** *An Imperial plate very similar to 73.* **83:** *The Scottish Union Insurance Company.* **86:** *Norwich Union. See 105.* **87:** *Compare with 62.* **88:** *A rare variant of the County Office. See 2.*

89: *British Commercial (1820).* **90, 92:** *West of England (Exeter, 1807) with King Alfred as an emblem.* **91:** *The Queen Insurance Company. See 45.* **93:** *Compare with 108.* **94:** *Etna (Dublin, 1866).* **95:** *Commercial Union with a salamander as an emblem. There was a separate Salamander office of 1803 (see 127) which used the same device.* **96:** *A British Commercial plate showing the caduceus of Hermes, god of peace.* **97:** *Scottish Imperial (Glasgow, 1865).* **98:** *Scottish Commercial (Glasgow, 1865) with the figure of Charity.*

Hands were of the greatest importance in fire fighting and they are an appropriate symbol to use on a fire-mark. There was an obvious significance in the clasped hands which became a very popular device. Care is often needed to distinguish between the many variants. The earliest marks bearing hands belong to the Hand-in-Hand Fire Office (London, 1696-1905). This shows a pair of clasped hands with a crown above. At the base there is a panel for the number (175, 176). Two pairs of clasped hands appear in a cruciform fashion on the marks and plates of the Union Assurance Society (London, 1714-1907), **99, 100, 102, 103, 106.** An alternative popular name for the Union Assurance Society was the Double Hand-in-Hand. The Friendly Insurance Society of Edinburgh (1720-1847), **5, 122,** also favoured the clasped hands. **101:** Plate of the Norwich Union. **104:** A lead mark of 'the Double Hand-in-Hand' issued before 1750. **105:** An unusual plate of the Norwich Union. Compare with 22-4, 37-9, 60, 61, 86 and 151. **107, 108:** Two plates of the Royal (Liverpool, 1845). One shows the liver bird which appears on 69 and 71. **109:** The Athenaeum can probably claim to have the fire-plate par excellence. There are at least five variants — four in porcelain and one in stoneware. These superb porcelain plates were probably made by James Dudson of Hanley (1838-88). The plates in the Chartered Institute's collection are of known dates, 1852 and 1856. This company had a very short existence. It was established in London in 1852 and was then in turn absorbed by the following — Times (1856), State (1858), Leeds and Yorkshire (1861), Liverpool and Globe (1864) and the Royal (1919).

16

99

100

101

102

103

104

105

106

107

108

109

110   111   112

113   114   115

110: *Britannia Fire Association (1868-79).* **111:** *The Great Britain (1871-80) has another use of St George.* **112:** *Equitable. See also 63.* **113:* *Economic Fire Insurance Company (1868-9).* **114:** *City of London (1881-92).* **115:** *Palatine Insurance Company. See also 66.*

116

117

118

119

120

121

116-117: *A large number of fire insurance companies borrowed their various emblems directly from heraldic sources associated with their place of origin. In certain cases civic arms were borrowed in their entirety. This was an infringement of heraldic propriety but no one seemed to object and hundreds of pirated escutcheons were manufactured. The Bath Fire Office (1767-1827) employed the popular version of the city arms which shows a castle wall with waves above. The sword of St Paul is also* present (in pale) to remind us of Bath's former abbey. It is easy to confuse the latter mark with that of the Bath Sun Fire Office (1776-1838), which used the same arms and a shield of almost identical shape with a heraldic sun above (144).

118: *Bath Fire Office plate.* **119:** *Salop Fire Office (1780-1890) with three leopards' heads derived from the civic arms.* **120, 121:** *Dundee Insurance Company (1782-1832) with a classical vase and three lilies.*

122

123

124

125

126

127

122: *Plate of the Friendly Insurance Society of Edinburgh. See also 5.* **123, 124:** *The London Assurance was established by Act of Parliament in 1720. Its seated female figure holds a harp in one hand and a spear in the other. A shield bearing the City of London arms also forms part of the design. These marks were issued (123) in 1723 and (124) in 1758. Compare them with 128-30 opposite.* **125, 126:** *A mark and a plate of the Dublin Insurance Company Against Fire (1782-c 1815). The design is based on the city arms.* **127:** *Salamander and Western Fire Assurance Society (1803-35). The salamander represents fire on the arms of the Chartered Insurance Institute.*

128

129

130

131

132

133

128: *An early copper plate of the London Assurance, probably about 1806.* **129, 130:** *These later plates show the usual figure of Britannia but have an extra feature, a burning* beacon. **131, 132:** *Two marks of the Bristol Fire Office (1769-1839). The ship emerging from the castle gateway is derived from the city arms.* **133:** *A circular variant of the Bristol Office.*

134

135

136

134-136: *Three variants of the Globe Insurance Company (1803-64). See also 69, 71 and 140.* **137-139:** *Plates of the Nottingham and Derbyshire Fire and Life Assurance Company (1835-69).* **140:** *Plate of the Liverpool and London and Globe. See 69, 71, 134-6.* **141-142:** *The Guardian was established in London in 1821 and it remained a separate company until 1968 when it was amalgamated with the Royal Exchange. The oldest variant is based upon a breastplate which is surmounted by Athena's head. The name Guardian appears on a curved label across the centre. Guardian plates of the keyhole type like those shown occur in much greater numbers and depict Athena armed with a spear. On the two variants here she also carries an olive branch.* **143:** *A Bath Sun plate. See also 158, 161, 162, 163.* **144:** *A Bath Sun mark which can easily be confused with 117.* **145:** *A Manchester Fire Office (1771-93) mark. The device is a lion passant on a heraldic*

wreath, which may be derived from John of Gaunt's crest. **146:** *One of the few designs to show a fire engine. The North British was established in Edinburgh in 1809.* **147:** *National Union (Bedford, 1894).* **148:** *An Alliance keyhole plate. See also 54, 72.* **149:** *Agriculture too has a place in the world of the fire-plate. The symbol of the Farmers' Company, later the Royal Farmers' Insurance Company (London, 1840-88), was a wheatsheaf.* **150:** *Berkshire, Gloucestershire and Provincial Life and Fire Insurance Company (1824-31). The building portrayed is probably Reading Castle, now demolished. At the base of the oval appears the motto 'Salus'.* **151:** *A circular plate of the Norwich Union. See 105.* **152:** *A Shropshire and North Wales (Shrewsbury, 1837-90) plate which made use of the Prince of Wales's feathers. This design is post-1840.* **153:** *The Caledonian Insurance Company (Edinburgh, 1805) used an established national emblem.*

137

138

139

140

141

142

143

144

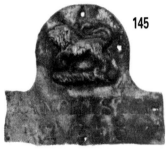

145

146

149

147

148

150

151

152

153

154 155

156 157

154: *Lion Fire Insurance Company (1879-1902).* **155:** *London Provincial (1881-1901).* **156:** *See 68.* **157:** *The Property Insurance* *Company (1898-1913) used a design which incorporates the emblems of England, Scotland and Ireland.*

24

158

159

160

161

162

163

164

165

166

167

168

169

158, 161-163: *The Sun Fire Office was established in London in 1710. It was one of the companies which maintained its own fire brigade. Early marks were made of lead and had the policy number displayed at the base. Eventually the circular plates were evolved and these can be seen in a variety of forms. There are twenty-six Sun variants.* **159:** *Albion (1805-28).* **160:** *A Norwich variant. See 105.* **164, 165:**

Beacon (1821-7) plates show Charity comforting a mother and child. There is a burning building in the background. Compare with 9 above. **166, 167:** *Later plates of the Royal Exchange (1720). The building portrayed is the second Royal Exchange which was destroyed by fire in 1838.* **168:** *A Birmingham Fire Office (1805-67) plate showing a fireman and engine.* **169:** *A Bristol mark. See 131.*

170: *The Insurance Company of Scotland (Edinburgh, 1821-47) displayed the Scottish crown and regalia on a cushion.* **171-173:** *National Assurance Company of Ireland (Dublin, 1822-1904). The shamrock was replaced by the crown and a harp.* **174:** *The oldest fire-mark known, The Friendly Society of London (1683-1790?). The design is probably derived from the arms of William Hale, of King's Walden, Hertfordshire, who was one of the company's promoters. See pages 4 and 9.* **175, 176:** *Hand-in-Hand Fire Office (1696-1905), which was also known in its early days as the*

Amicable Contributorship; the clasped hands also appear on other marks and plates. Compare with 5, 60, 61, 99, 100, 104. **177-179:** *Hibernian marks and a plate. See also 55.* **180, 181:** *Liverpool Fire Office (1777-95). The device is the liver bird taken from the city arms. See also 140 above.* **182:** *General Insurance Company of Ireland (Dublin, 1779-1824). This mark portrays a phoenix rising from a heraldic wreath. Compare it with the Phoenix mark (185) below.* **183, 184:** *Variants of the Dundee marks. See also 120, 121.*

177   178   179

180   181   182

183   184   185

186

187

188

POSTSCRIPT

Fire-marks and plates still adorn the walls of thousands of buildings. But their number is gradually diminishing as old buildings are demolished or refurbished, and these fascinating signs can now often be found on sale in antique dealers' shops. Very early marks can be expensive, particularly if their provenance is known and there is documentary evidence to support their history. Fake marks seem to have been produced too. Some spurious marks are now quite ancient. It is not easy to detect an old reproduction and there are no set rules for identification. The presence of a mark on any building is not a guarantee that it was originally placed there. Old marks can find new homes on other walls.

Occasionally the marks of two companies will be found on the house. This may indicate that the building was re-insured at some stage. Rows of houses bearing a set of identical marks will sometimes be found. Such circumstances could indicate a cautious landlord who insured all his property, which was then marked with individual plates.

For those with an eye for such things there is still a lot to see and there are many minor puzzles to untangle.

186: *Fireman's badge of the Atlas Assurance Company (1808).* **187:** *Fireman's badge of the Protector Fire Insurance Company. See 11, 12 above.* **188:** *One of the splendid oval marks of the Royal Exchange. See 166, 167.*

LIST OF FIRE OFFICES AND VARIANTS

Established	Number of variants	Materials L=lead · c=copper · f=iron b=brass · tp=tin plate · ft=tinned iron
1683 The Friendly Society of London	2	2L
1696 Hand-in-Hand	12	10L, 2c
1710 Sun Fire Office	26	19L, 5c, 2f
1714 Union Society	13	3L, 6c, 4f
1717 Westminster Fire Office	11	6L, 3c, 2f
1718 The Bristol Crown Fire Office	4	4L
1720 Friendly Insurance Society of Edinburgh	10	8L, 2f
1720 Friendly Insurance Society of Glasgow	1	1L
1720 The London Assurance	16	10L, 4c, 2f
1720 Royal Exchange Assurance	13	12L, 1c
1767 Bath Fire Office	4	3L, 1c
1769 Bristol Fire Office	5	2L, 3c
1771 Hibernian Fire Insurance Company	5	5L
1771 Manchester Fire Office	1	1L
1774 Bristol Universal Fire Office	2	2L
1776 Bath Sun Fire Office	4	3L, 1c
1777 Leeds Fire Office	1	1L
1777 Liverpool Fire Office	2	2L
1779 General Insurance Company of Ireland	4	3L, 1f
1780 Salop Fire Office	2	1L, 1c
1782 Dundee Insurance Company	5	4L, 1 sheet iron
1782 Dublin Insurance Company Against Fire	4	4L
1782 Phoenix Assurance Company	15	3L, 10c, 2f
1783 Newcastle upon Tyne Fire Office	4	3L, 1c
1784 Royal Exchange of Ireland	1	1L
1790 Worcester Fire Office	4	3L, 1f
1792 Norwich General Assurance Office	5	4L, 1c
1797 Norwich Union Fire Insurance Society	21	2L, 9c, 10f
1799 British Fire Office	7	3L, 4c
1799 Commercial Fire Insurance Company of Dublin	2	1L, 1f
1800 Fife Insurance Company	1	1ft
1801 Aberdeen Fire Assurance Office	1	1L
1802 Essex and Suffolk Equitable Insurance Society	1	1c
1802 Kent Fire Insurance Company	5	2L, 3c
1802 Suffolk and General Counties Insurance Office	4	3L, 1c
1802 Sun Insurance Company of Dublin	1	1L
1803 Globe Insurance Company	5	2c, 3f
1803 Hants, Sussex and Dorset Fire Office	2	1c, 1b
1803 Imperial Fire Insurance Company	7	4c, 3f
1804 British and Irish United	3	2c, 1ft
1805 Albion Fire and Life Insurance Company	1	1f
1805 Birmingham Fire Office Company	6	4c, 1b, 1f
1805 Caledonian Insurance Company	4	3c, 1f
1805 Glasgow Insurance Company	3	3L
1807 Eagle Insurance Company	6	1L, 2c, 3f
1807 Hope Fire and Life Assurance Company	4	2c, 2f
1807 County Fire Office	12	9c, 2f, 1 zinc
1807 West of England Fire and Life Assurance Company	11	8c, 3f
1808 Anchor Fire Office	1	1c
1808 Atlas Assurance Company	1	1c
1808 Sheffield Fire Office	2	2tp
1809 Hercules Insurance Company	2	2f

Established	Number of variants	Materials L=lead b=brass c=copper tp=tin plate f=iron ft=tinned iron
1809 North British and Mercantile Insurance Company	7	3c, 4f
1818 British Union Fire and Life Insurance Company	2	1c, 1f
1820 British Commercial Life and Fire Insurance Company	3	1L, 2c
1821 Beacon Fire Insurance Company	3	3c
1821 Guardian Assurance Company	4	4c
1821 Insurance Company of Scotland	1	1c
1822 National Assurance Company of Ireland	5	1c, 4f
1822 Reading Insurance Company	1	1c
1822 Salamander and Western Fire Assurance Society	4	1L, 2c, 1b
1823 Royal Irish Assurance Company	2	1c, 1L
1823 Shamrock Fire and Life Assurance Company	1	1L
1824 Alliance Assurance Company	6	5c, 1f
1824 Irish Alliance Insurance Company	1	1f
1824 Berkshire, Gloucester and Provincial Life and Fire Insurance Company	1	1c
1824 East Kent and Canterbury Economic Fire Assurance Association	1	1ft
1824 Essex Economic Fire Office	2	2c
1824 Herts, Cambridge and County Fire Office	4	3c, 1f
1824 Leeds and Yorkshire Assurance Company	2	1c, 1f
1824 Manchester Fire Insurance Company	6	2c, 4f
1824 Palladium	1	1c
1824 Patriotic Assurance Company of Ireland	9	1L, 2c, 1b, 5f
1824 Scottish Union Insurance Company	5	4c, 1ft
1824 St Patrick Insurance Company	1	1c
1824 Yorkshire Insurance Company	4	3c, 1f
1825 Aberdeen Assurance Company	3	1L, 1c, 1f
1825 Aegis Fire and Life Insurance Company	1	1c
1825 Protector	2	2c
1825 Surrey, Sussex and Southwark Fire Assurance Company	1	1c
1825 Sussex County and General Fire and Life Assurance Company	1	1c
1826 West of Scotland Insurance Office	2	2L
1834 District Fire Office	8	6c, 1b, 1ft
1834 Leicester Fire and Life Insurance Company	1	1f
1834 York and North of England Assurance Company	3	2c, 1f
1835 Notts and Derbyshire Fire and Life Assurance Company	12	9c, 3 zinc
1836 Licensed Victuallers Fire and Life Assurance Company	3	3c
1836 (Liverpool and London)	2	1c, 1f
(Liverpool and London and Globe)	2	2c
1836 Northern Assurance Company	5	3c, 2f
1837 General Life and Fire Assurance Company	1	1f
1837 Shropshire and North Wales Assurance Company	3	1c, 2b
1840 Royal Farmers and General Fire, Life and Hailstorm Insurance Company	5	3c, 2 zinc
1840 Church of England Life and Fire Assurance Institute	2	2c
1841 Winchester, Hants and South of England Fire and Life Insurance Company	2	2c
1845 Royal Insurance Company	11	5c, 6f
1845 Star Fire Insurance Company	2	2c

Established	Number of variants	Materials L=lead b=brass c=copper tp=tin plate f=iron ft=tinned iron
1849 Anchor Fire and Life Insurance Company	1	1f
1852 Athenaeum Fire Insurance Company	5	4 porcelain, 1 stoneware
1852 Lancashire Insurance Company	4	3c, 1f
1857 Queen Insurance Company	5	2c, 1b, 2ft
1861 Commercial Union Assurance Company	4	4f
1862 London and Lancashire Insurance Company	6	3c, 3f
1864 Albert Insurance Company	1	1c
1865 Scottish Commercial Fire and Life Insurance Company	1	1c
1865 Scottish Imperial Insurance Company	1	1c
1866 Etna Insurance Company	1	1f
1868 Economic Fire Insurance Company	1	1c
1868 Britannia Fire Association	1	1c
1871 Great Britain Company	1	1c
1873 Equitable Fire Insurance Company	2	2c
1874 Middlesex Fire Insurance Company	1	1f
1878 National Fire Insurance Corporation	2	1c, 1f
1879 Lion Fire Insurance Company	1	1c
1881 London and Provincial Fire Insurance Company	1	1f
1881 City of London Fire	1	1f
1886 Palatine Insurance Company	2	1c, 1f
1887 Western Insurance Company of Plymouth	1	1f
1894 National Union Fire Office	1	
1895 Empress Assurance Corporation	1	1c
1896 National British and Irish Millers' Insurance Company	2	2f
1898 Property Insurance Company	1	1f
1899 Central Insurance Company	1	1c
1905 London and Westminster Insurance Company	1	1f
1907 Monarch Insurance Company	1	1c

The author will be pleased to receive any additions to the above list.

FURTHER READING

Baumer, Edward. *The Early Days of the Sun Fire Office*. Sun, 1910.
Briggs, Geoffrey. *Civic and Corporate Heraldry*. Heraldry Today, 1971.
Chartered Insurance Institute. *British Firemarks and Plates: A Catalogue of the Institute and Bashall Dawson Collections*. 1971.
Dickson, P. G. M. *The Sun Insurance Office 1710 - 1960*. Oxford University Press, 1960.
Kirk, John L. (editor). *History of Firefighting*. City of York Castle Museum, 1960.
Williams, Bertram. *Specimens of British Fire Marks*. Layton, 1934.
Wright, Brian. *The British Fire Mark 1680-1879*. Woodhead-Faulkner, 1982.
Wright, Brian. *Firefighting Equipment*. Shire, 1989.

PLACES TO VISIT

Belvoir Castle, Grantham, Lincolnshire. Telephone: 0476 870262.
Bridgnorth Museum, North Gate, High Street, Bridgnorth, Shropshire.
City of Bristol Museum and Art Gallery, Queens Road, Bristol BS8 1RL. Telephone: 0272 299771.
Derby Museum and Art Gallery, The Strand, Derby. Telephone: 0332 31111 extension 782.
Mary Arden's House, Wilmcote, Stratford-upon-Avon, Warwickshire. Telephone: 0789 204016.
Museum of London, London Wall, London EC2Y 5HN. Telephone: 01-600 3699.
Reading Museum and Art Gallery, Blagrave Street, Reading, Berkshire. Telephone: 0734 55911 extension 2242.
St Albans Museum, Hatfield Road, St Albans, Hertfordshire. Telephone 0727 56679.
Waterways Museum, Stoke Bruerne, Towcester, Northamptonshire. Telephone: 0604 862229.
York Castle Museum, Tower Street, York YO1 1RY. Telephone: 0904 653611.

THE FIREMARK CIRCLE
Hon. Secretary: David H. Wesson, FCII, Royal Insurance (UK) Ltd, New Hall Place, Liverpool L69 3EN. Telephone: 051-227 4422 extension 3694.

THE CHARTERED INSURANCE INSTITUTE
The Institute is the professional association for all those engaged in insurance. Its headquarters are at 20 Aldermanbury, London EC2V 7HY, telephone 01-606 3835. From here it carries out the three functions for which it exists, educational, social and benevolent. It has branches and affiliates throughout the United Kingdom, the Republic of Ireland and the rest of the world. The Institute owes its origin to a group of Manchester insurance men who formed a society in 1873 to promote professional standards. A federation of similar societies was established in 1897. The Institute received its Royal Charter in 1912. Its splendid hall in Aldermanbury was one of the few buildings in the area to survive the London Blitz.

Replica fire-marks and plates are available from the Secretary (Technical) at the Institute.

ACKNOWLEDGEMENTS
The author expresses his appreciation to the Chartered Insurance Institute, which allowed its splendid collections of marks and plates to be photographed and provided information concerning their history. Other marks illustrated are in the private collection of Mr Leslie Harris, a member of the Firemark Circle, who has also supplied additional information. Special thanks are due to Mr P. V. Saxton for his expert help and advice and to the Firemark Circle. The photograph of the Monument is by Robert D. Bristow. The cover illustration is reproduced by courtesy of the Buckinghamshire County Museum, Aylesbury,